You Can't Stop Me

Allison Aller

Illustrated by: Nadia Asfand Yar

Copyright © 2024 by Allison Aller

All rights reserved.

No portion of this book may be reproduced in any form without written permission from the publisher or author, except as permitted by U.S. copyright law.

ISBN: 979-8-218-34258-6

Book Cover and Illustrations by Techphics.
Techphics WhatsApp Contact: 92-314-8004883

To my loud, bossy, emotional, and intelligent baby girl; no one, and nothing, can stop you. You are my inspiration.

Thank you to my tough, opinionated, and loving Mom who raised me to be as headstrong and she is. You give me strength.

Thank you to my kind, strong, and crazy Grandma who has always encouraged me in every chapter of my life. You taught me to always follow my dreams.

They told her to keep her opinions to herself,
that her words won't inspire a thing.
They said, "Your story only matters to yourself."
She said, "You can't stop me."

So, she wrote and published her first book.
It's her favorite on her shelf.

If only she knew this is all it took
to change the world herself.

So, she joined the debate team,
and she won every round.
She was so excited, she started to scream,
"I'm the best talker in town!"

So, she ran and was elected president,
the biggest boss of all.

She was never crazy, just confident,
that she could make a difference for all.

So, she started her own clothing line, and wow, did it blow everyone away. She never knew that her own design could end up on the runway.

They told her she wasn't strong enough to play with the guys,
that she was too weak for the team.
They told her if she made it, it would be a surprise.
She said, "You can't stop me."

So, she made the soccer team,
and she even became captain.
She did the extreme.
She always knew she could make this happen.

They told her she wasn't very smart,
that it's such a waste to study.
They said, "You won't beat us, sweetheart."
She said, "You can't stop me."

So, she entered her school's spelling bee,
and took home first place.
She just couldn't wait to see,
her new trophy on her bookcase.

So, she went to the soup kitchen and helped feed her neighborhood. When she's put in a giving position, it makes her feel oh, so good.

They told her she'd live in a small town forever, that a small-town girl is all she'd ever be. They said no one's made it out, ever. She said, "You can't stop me."

So, she left her small town, all right.
She went all the way to the moon.

She always knew her future was bright
and that she'd be an astronaut so soon.

We are a forceful team. That, we've proven to be.

Together, we powerfully scream, "You can't stop me!"

Copyright © 2024 by Allison Aller

www.ingramcontent.com/pod-product-compliance
Lightning Source LLC
Chambersburg PA
CBHW060411010526
44107CB00006B/654